FINGERPICKING BEATLES

The songs appear in this book according to playing level with the easiest arrangements first.

P9-AFT-600

4 Introduction

5 How To Read Chord Grids

5 About Fingerpicking

6 How To Read Tablature

7 Chord Dictionary

32 And I Love Her

62 Come Together

19 Eight Days A Week

42 Eleanor Rigby

29 Girl

26 Here Comes The Sun

47 Here, There and Everywhere

59 Hey Jude

50 If I Fell

12 In My Life

10 Let It Be

56 Lucy In The Sky With Diamonds

22 Michelle

24 Norwegian Wood [This Bird Has Flown]

35 Something

53 Strawberry Fields Forever

15 When I'm Sixty-Four

44 While My Guitar Gently Weeps

38 With A Little Help From My Friends

8 Yesterday

Introduction

The Beatles broadened the scope of pop music by blending virtually all forms of music: R&B, blues, rock, pop ballads, country, rockabilly, classical, Indian music, English Music Hall and American folk. Their studio recording innovations forever changed the way pop music is recorded. They were *the* biggest musical influence of the '60s and their recordings continue to inspire rock, country, R&B and folk musicians all over the world.

This collection of tunes shows the variety of the Beatles' repertoire. They began in the early '60s with simple rock/pop songs like "She Loves You" and "Eight Days A Week" and pretty ballads like "If I Fell" (which could be a '40s tune). Just a few years later they were recording psychedelic musical collages like "Strawberry Fields Forever" and "Lucy In The Sky With Diamonds," both of which contain several changes of key, time signature, and texture and were awash in sitars, harpsichords, hurdy-gurdys, symphonic strings, feedback guitars and phased, sped-up and slowed-down instruments and vocal tracks!

Though the Beatles music evolved and changed during their twelve-year career, their LPs (those big vinyl discs) always included memorable melodies—tunes you could hum! Songs with strong melodies have long lives, and *they are easy to play on the guitar*. The twenty-one Beatles tunes in this collection are so melodic that the fairly simple fingerpicking versions are very pretty and complete.

These arrangements are solo adaptations for the beginning-to-intermediate player, although melodies and lyrics have also been included. There are a few barred chords and up-the-neck licks, but most of the playing is on the first four or five frets and most of the chords are easy, first-position chords. It's all written in tablature and music notation, and there are chord grids whenever an *unusual* chord appears. **The order of the songs in this book is according to playing level, with the easiest arrangements first.**

Whether these songs are new to you or nostalgic, they're fun to play and full of musical surprises...and they're a great way to improve your finger-style guitar picking.

Good Luck!

Fred Sokolow

FINGERPICKING BEATLES

Arranged by Fred Sokolow

ISBN 0-7935-3082-2

HAL•LEONARD™
CORPORATION

7777 W. BLUEMOUND RD. P.O. BOX 13819 MILWAUKEE, WI 53213

How To Read Chord Grids

A *chord grid* is a picture of three or four frets of the guitar's fretboard. The dots show you where to fret (finger) the strings:

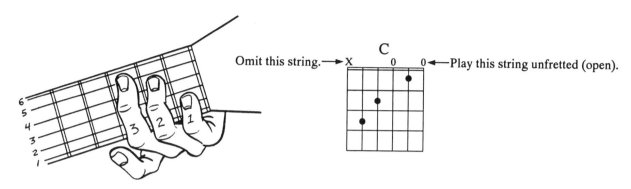

Omit this string. → X   C   0   0 ←— Play this string unfretted (open).

Numbers below the grid indicate the fingering. The number to the right of the grid is a *fret number*.

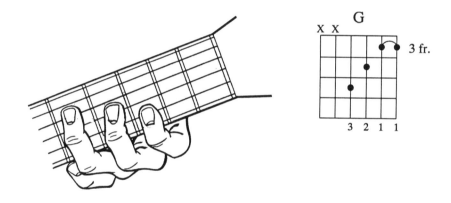

G
X X
3 fr.
3 2 1 1

About Fingerpicking

In blues, rock, country and folk fingerpicking, the thumb usually picks the *bass line* on the lower strings while the index and middle finger play *melody* on the top (treble) strings. The arrangements in this book are based on this tradition. Sometimes the bass line resembles what Paul McCartney played, and sometimes the melody line includes a harmony part similar to the Beatles' vocal harmony.

All the tunes are written in tablature and standard music notation. In standard notation...

- Notes that are plucked by the thumb have stems pointing down.

- Notes picked by the fingers have stems pointing up.

How To Read Tablature

Songs, scales and exercises in this book are written in standard music notation and tablature. The six lines of the tablature staff represent the six guitar strings:

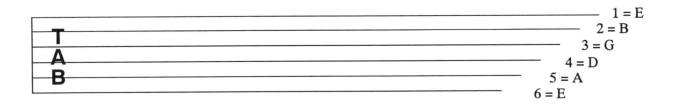

1 = E
2 = B
3 = G
4 = D
5 = A
6 = E

A number on a line tells you which string to play and where to fret it.

This example means "play the 3rd string on the 4th fret"

This example means "play the 4th string unfretted"

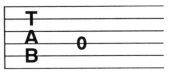

Chords can also be written in tablature:

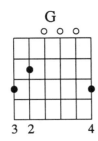

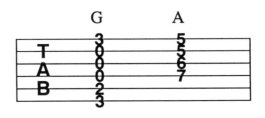

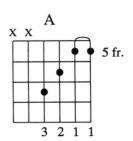

Chord Dictionary

Most of the chords used in this book are basic, first-position chords. Here they are, with suggested fingerings. Less common chords are written out *in the arrangments* in the form of music, tablature, and grids, and they are listed with their fingerings before the tune in which they occur.

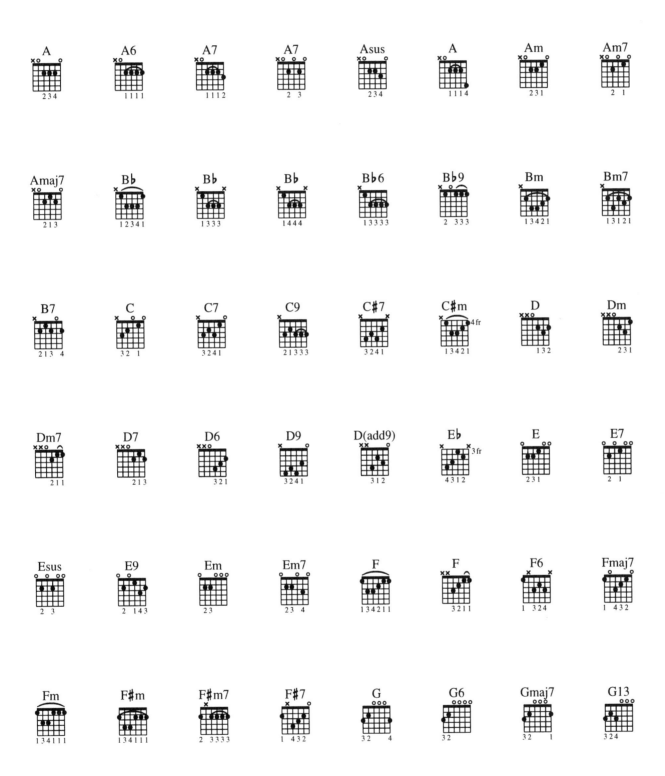

Yesterday

Words and Music by John Lennon and Paul McCartney

The arrangement features many two-note chords that consist of a bass note and melody note. Notice the ascending melody line and descending bass line in the second bar of the bridge. Here are two unusual chord shapes:

F#m11

B

yes - ter - day.___
sud - den - ly.___
yes - ter - day. ___

Why she had to go, I don't know, she would - n't say._

I said some - thing wrong, now I long for yes - ter -

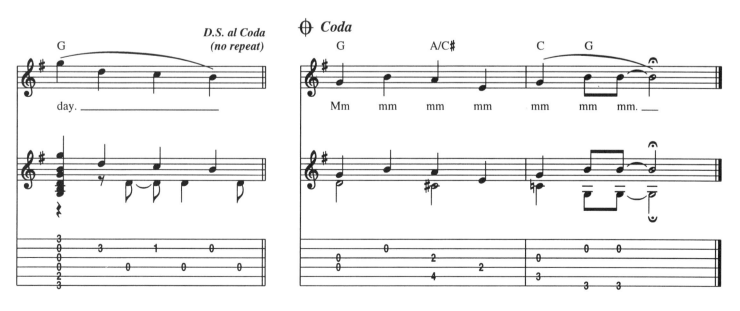

day. ___

Mm mm mm mm mm mm mm. ___

Let It Be

Words and Music by John Lennon and Paul McCartney

Even in this simple arrangement, which uses first position chords, the gospel flavor of the song comes across.

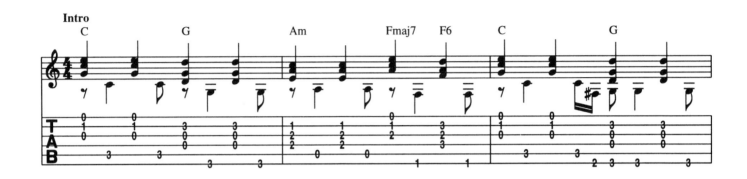

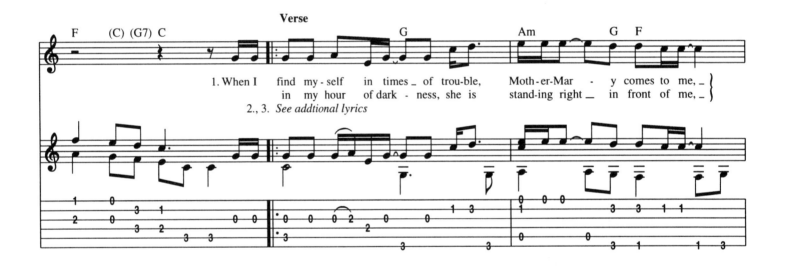

1. When I find my-self in times of trou-ble, Moth-er-Mar - y comes to me, }
   in my hour of dark - ness, she is stand-ing right in front of me, }
   2., 3. *See additional lyrics*

speak-ing words of wis - dom, let it be. And be. Let it be,

MCA music publishing

Additional Lyrics

And when the brokenhearted people living in the world agree,
There will be answer, let it be.
For though they may be parted, there is still a chance that they will see.
There will be an answer, let it be. *(Chorus)*

And when the night is cloudy, there is still a light that shines on me.
Shine until tomorrow, let it be.
I wake up to the sound of music, Mother Mary comes to me,
Speaking words of wisdom, let it be. *(Chorus)*

In My Life

Words and Music by John Lennon and Paul McCartney

Here are some unusual chord shapes:

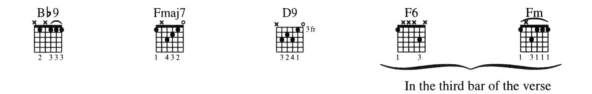

In the third bar of the verse

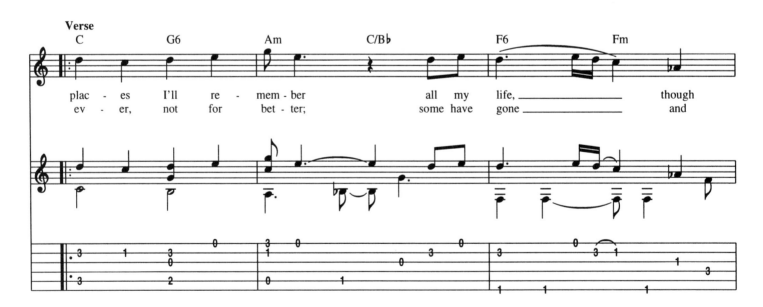

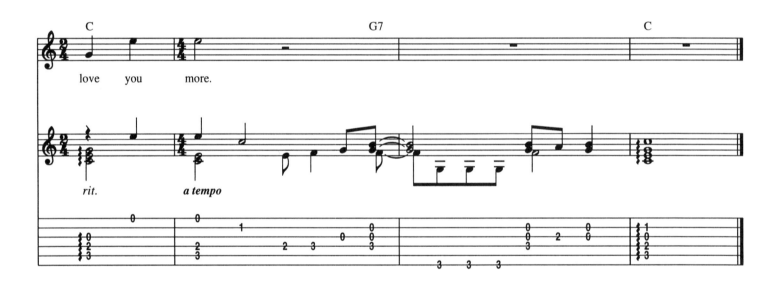

Additional Lyrics

2. But of all these friends and lovers, there is no one compared with you.
   And these mem'ries lose their meaning when I think of love as something new.

   (Chorus)

   Though I know I'll never lose affection for people and things that went before,
   I know I'll often stop and think about them, in my life I love you more.
   In my life I love you more.

When I'm Sixty-Four

Words and Music By John Lennon and Paul McCartney

Make sure you know these chords:

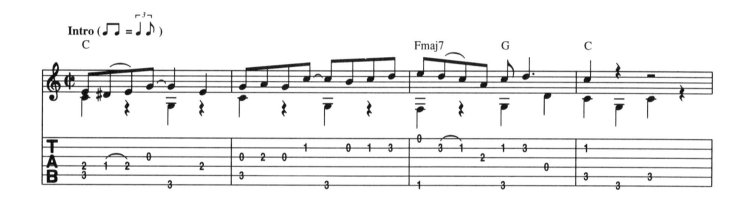

1. When I get old - er, los - ing my hair, ___ man - y years from now, ___
2.,3. *See additional lyrics*

will you still be send-ing me a val-en - tine, _ birth - day greet - ings, bot - tle of wine? _

If I've been out _ 'til quar-ter to three, _ would you lock the door? _

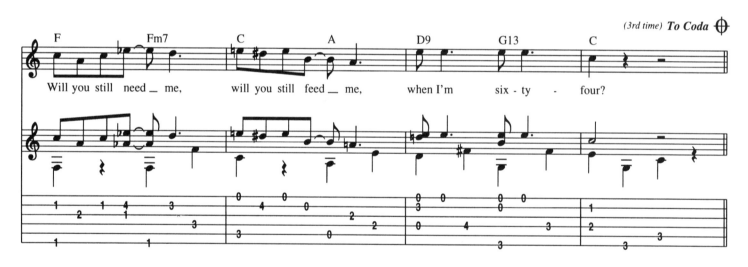

Will you still need _ me, will you still feed _ me, when I'm six - ty - four?

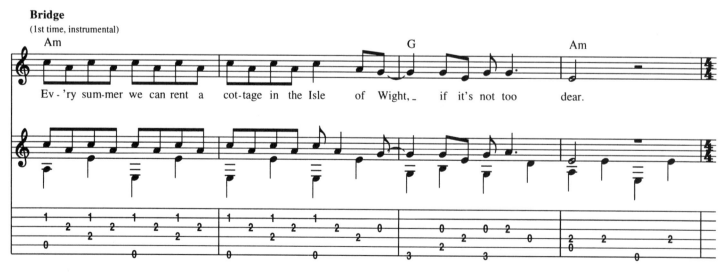

Bridge
(1st time, instrumental)

Ev - 'ry sum-mer we can rent a cot-tage in the Isle of Wight, _ if it's not too dear.

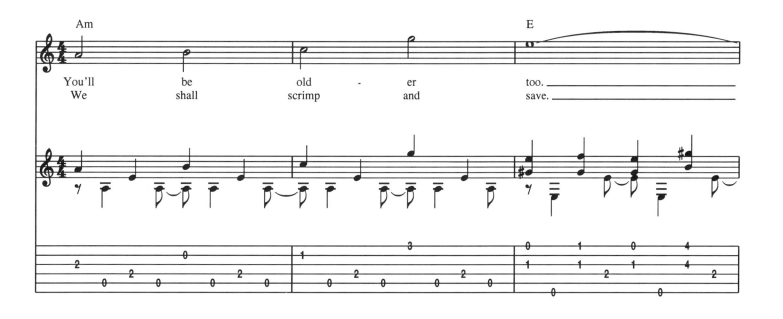

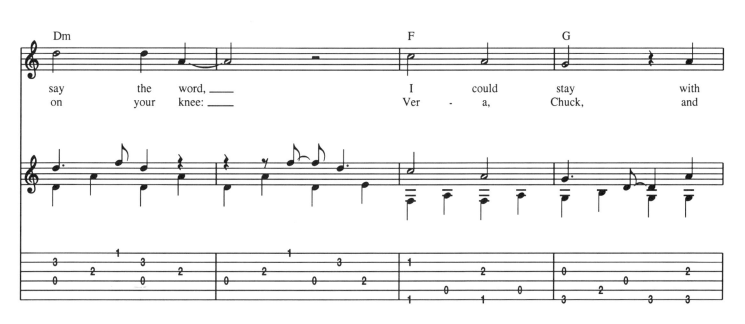

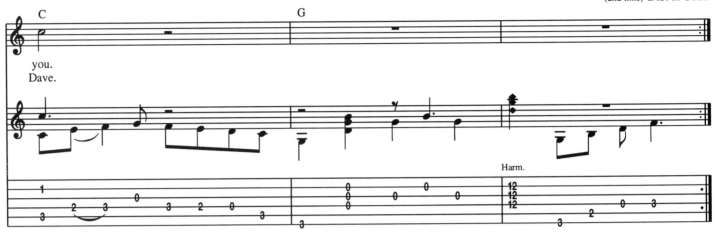

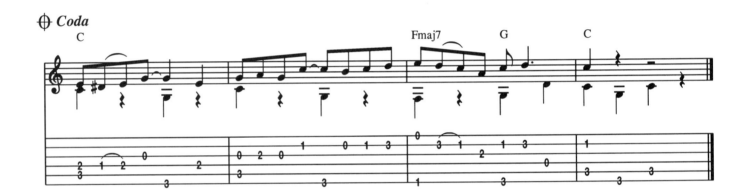

Additional Lyrics

2. I could be handy, mending a fuse when your lights have gone.
   You can knit a sweater by the fireside, Sunday morning go for a ride.
   Doing the garden, digging the weeds, who could ask for more?
   Will you still need me, will you still feed me, when I'm sixty-four?

3. Send me a postcard, drop me a line, stating point of view.
   Indicate precisely what you mean to say. Yours, sincerely, wasting away.
   Give me your answer, fill in a form: Mine forevermore.
   Will you still need me, will you still feed me, when I'm sixty-four? Ho!

Eight Days A Week

Words and Music By John Lennon and Paul McCartney

The "intro" and "outro" is a Buddy Holly-esque chord solo in which the first string is played unfretted, so that it drones throughout the four bars. Try this fingering for the three chords:

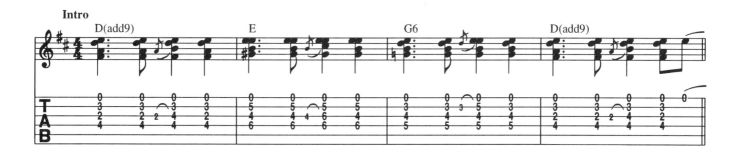

MCA music publishing

Chorus

Hold me, __ love me, __ hold me, __ love me. __ I

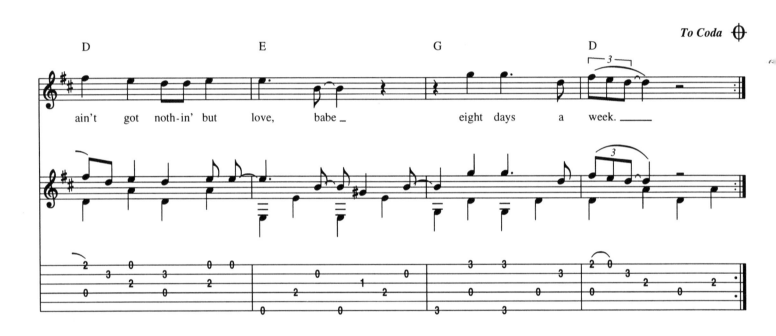

To Coda ⊕

ain't got noth-in' but love, babe __ eight days a week. ____

Bridge

Eight days a week I love _____ you. __

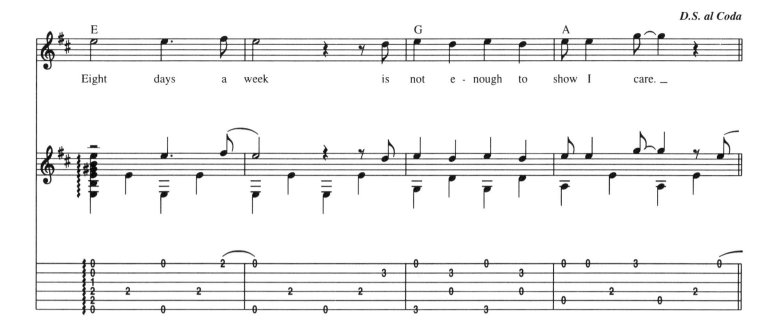

Eight days a week is not e - nough to show I care. __

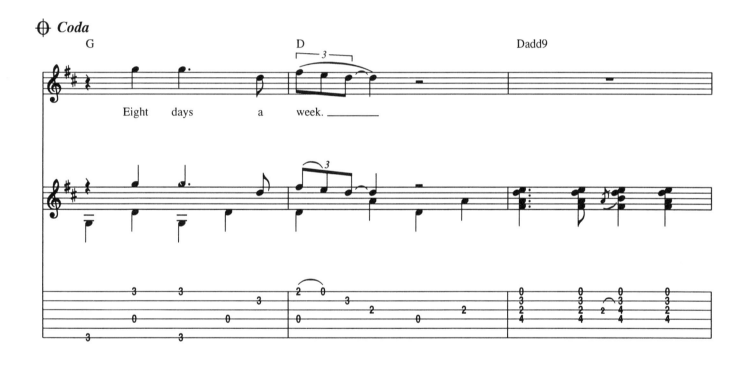

Coda

Eight days a week. _____

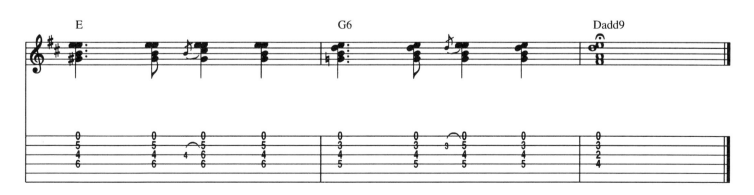

Michelle

Words and Music by John Lennon and Paul McCartney

Here are the fingerings for the unusual chord shapes in this tune:

Additional Lyrics

Michelle, ma belle, sont les mots qui vont tres bien ensemble, tres bien ensemble.

I need to, I need to, I need to, I need to make you see,
Oh, what you mean to me. Until I do, I'm hoping you will know what I mean.
I love you.

I want you, I want you, I want you. I think you know by now,
I'll get to you somehow. Until I do, I'm telling you, so you'll understand.

Michelle, ma belle, sont les mots qui vont tres bien ensemble, tres bien ensemble.
And I will say the only words I know that you'll understand, my Michelle.

Norwegian Wood (This Bird Has Flown)

Words and Music by John Lennon and Paul McCartney

As in "Hey Jude," this arrangement starts with three-note chords that are really two treble notes plus an open bass string. The 6th String "Drop D" tuning gives you these chord shapes:

Additional Lyrics

2. I sat on her rug, biding my time, drinking her wine.
   We talked until two, and then she said, "It's time for bed." *(Bridge)*

   She told me she worked in the morning and started to laugh.
   I told her I didn't and crawled off to sleep in the bath.

3. And when I awoke I was alone, this bird had flown.
   So I lit the fire, isn't it good Norwegian wood?

Here Comes The Sun

By George Harrison

If you capo up seven frets, you can play this arrangement with the Beatles recording. It's very similar to what George Harrison played on acoustic guitar. In spite of the drop-D tuning (see "Come Together"), the chord shapes are familiar... except for E7 and G:

This fingering of G allows you to play many variations:

Additional Lyrics

2. Little darling, the smile's returning to their faces;
   Little darling, it seems like years since it's been here. *(Chorus)*

3. Little darling, I feel that ice is slowly melting;
   Little darling, it seems like years since it's been clear. *(Chorus)*

Girl

Words and Music By John Lennon and Paul McCartney

To Play the B♭6 and B♭ chords at the end of the Bridge, use these fingerings:

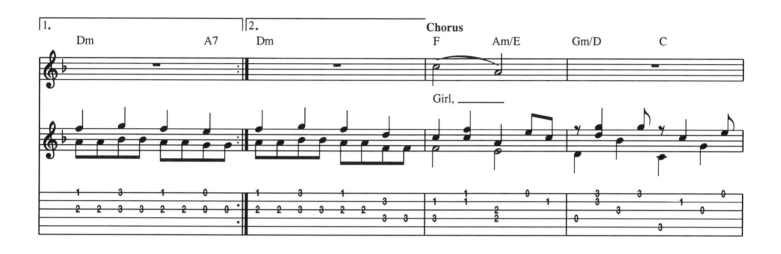

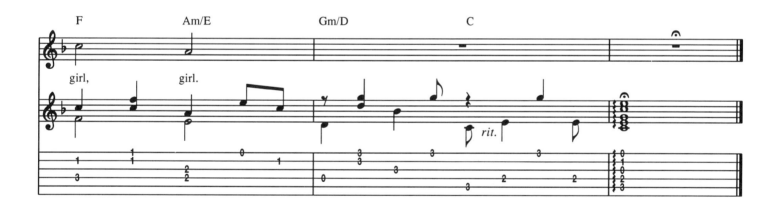

Additional Lyrics

2. When I think of all the times I tried so hard to leave her,
   She will turn to me and start to cry.
   And she promises the earth to me and I believe her,
   After all this time, I don't know why. *(Chorus)*

3. Was she told when she was young that pain would lead to pleasure?
   Did she understand it when they said
   That a man must break his back to earn his day of leisure?
   Will she still believe it when he's dead? *(Chorus)*

And I Love Her

Words and Music by John Lennon and Paul McCartney

This arrangement leaves the first position twice:

-The Am9 chord 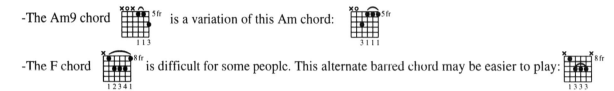 is a variation of this Am chord:

-The F chord is difficult for some people. This alternate barred chord may be easier to play:

Here's a good way to finger the seventh bar of the verse: Start with a one-finger barre, then add the rest of the F chord:

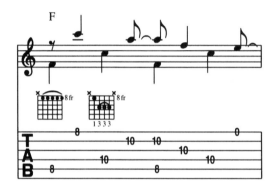

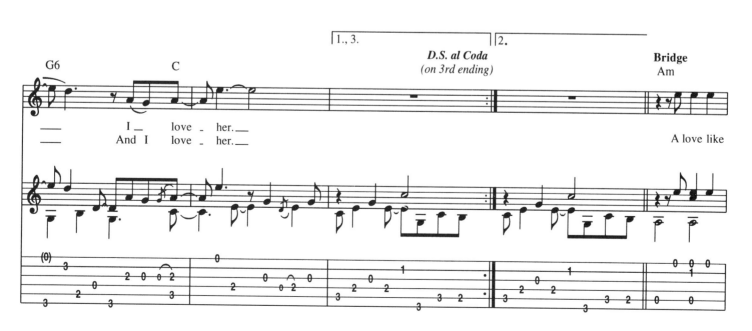

ours · · · could nev - er die, ___

To 3rd Verse

as long as I ___ have you near me.

⊕ Coda

Additional Lyrics

3. Bright are the stars that shine, dark is the sky.
I know this love of mine will never die, and I love her.

Something

By George Harrison

Here are some chord fingerings:

1. Some-thing in the way ___ she moves ___
2. Some-where in her smile ___ she knows ___
3. *See additional lyrics*

at - tracts ___ me like no oth - er lov-er. _____
that I ___ don't need no oth - er lov-er. _____

Something in the way ___ she woos ___
Something in her style ___ that shows.

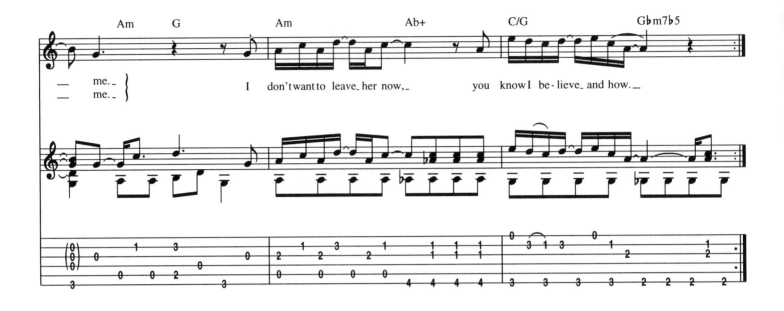

I don't want to leave her now, you know I believe and how.

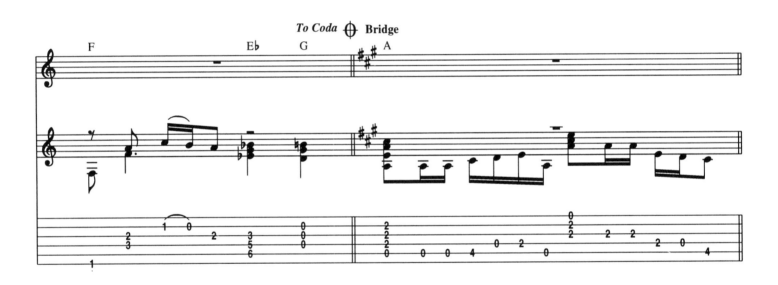

To Coda ⊕ **Bridge**

You're ask-ing me will my love grow,
You stick a-round now, it may show,

I don't know, I don't

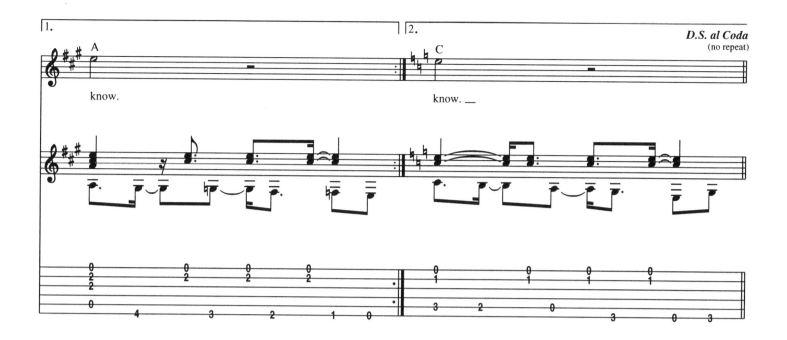

Additional Lyrics

3. Something in the way she knows, and all I have to do is think of her.
   Something in the things she shows me.
   I don't want to leave her now. You know I believe and how.

With A Little Help From My Friends

Words and Music by John Lennon and Paul McCartney

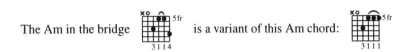

The Am in the bridge ⬚ is a variant of this Am chord: ⬚

B♭ can often be abbreviated to this two- or three-finger chord: ⬚

To play the bar of A♭ near the end of the Coda, use this fingering.
Keep your ring and little fingers in place while the bass notes change. ⬚

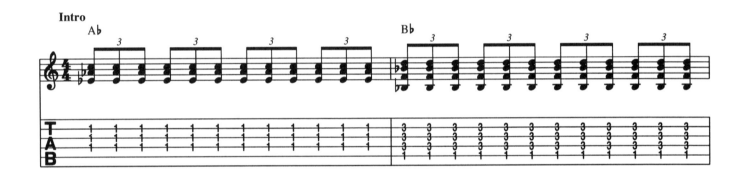

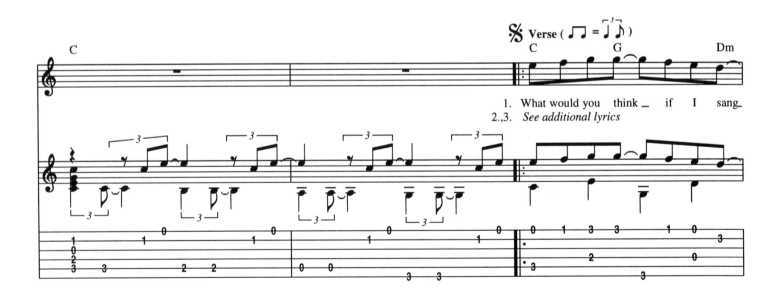

MCA music publishing

⊕ *Coda*

Additional Lyrics

2. What do I do when my love is away? (Does it worry you to be alone?)
   How do I feel by the end of the day? (Are you sad because you're on your own?)
   No, I get by etc. *(Chorus)*

3. (Would you believe in a love at first sight?) Yes, I'm certain that it happens all the time.
   (What do you see when you turn out the light?) I can't tell you, but I know it's mine.
   (Chorus)

Eleanor Rigby

Words and Music by John Lennon and Paul McCartney

MCA music publishing

Additional Lyrics

2. Father McKenzie, writing the words of a sermon that no one will hear,

   No one comes near.

   Look at him working, darning his socks in the night when there's nobody there,

   What does he care? *(2nd Chorus)*

3. Eleanor Rigby died in the church and was buried along with her name,

   Nobody came.

   Father McKenzie, wiping the dirt from his hands as he walks from the grave,

   No one was saved. *(2nd Chorus)*

While My Guitar Gently Weeps

By George Harrison

Here are the fingerings for some unusual chords:

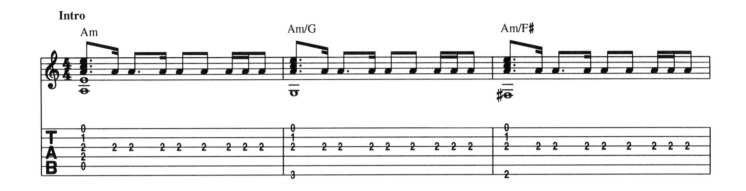

-ing, while
-ing, still } my guit - tar ___ gent - ly weeps. ___

I ___ gent - ly weeps. ___

Bridge

I don't_ know why _____ no-bod - y told ___ you
I don't_ know how _____ some-one__ con - trolled_ you;

how to __ un - fold __ your __ love. __
they bought and _ sold __ you. __

2nd time:

2. I

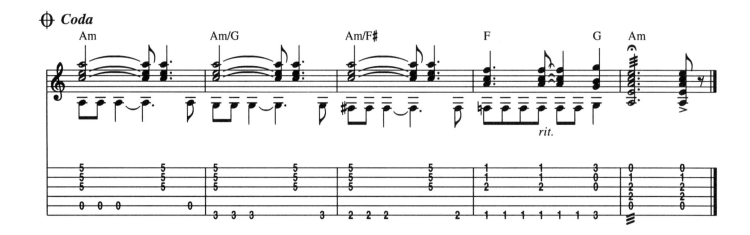

Additional Lyrics

2. I look at the world and I notice it's turning, while my guitar gently weeps.
   For every mistake, we must surely be learning. Still my guitar gently weeps.

   I don't know how you were diverted, you were perverted, too.
   I don't know how you were inverted, no one alerted you.

3. I look at you all, see the love there that's sleeping, while my guitar gently weeps.
   Look at you all ... still my guitar gently weeps.

Here, There And Everywhere

Words and Music by John Lennon and Paul McCartney

This is a fairly easy arrangement if you know the chord formations. Make sure these chords are familiar before you begin:

of her hand, no-bod-y can de-ny that there's some - thing there.

Bridge

I want her ev-'ry-where, and if she's be-side me, I know I need

D.S. al Coda

nev - er care. But to love her is to need her 3. ev-'ry-where,

Coda

Additional Lyrics

2. There, running my hands through her hair, both of us thinking how good it can be.
   Someone is speaking, but she doesn't know he's there.

3. Everywhere, knowing that love is to share, each one believing that love never dies,
   Watching her eyes and hoping I'm always there. *(Bridge)*

If I Fell

Words and Music by John Lennon and Paul McCartney

Like pop songs from the pre-rock era, this tune has an introduction that "sets up" the main part of the song. This is an especially clever intro because it is in a different key than the rest of the song; it's in E♭ and it modulates (changes keys) to E.

Like "Here, There And Everywhere," this is a fairly simple arrangement for a "chordy" tune. Review the less familiar chord shapes before playing it:

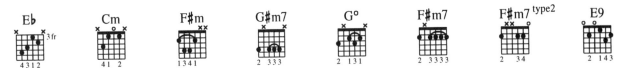

John Lennon and Paul McCartney sang very memorable harmony throughout this song, and it's recreated in this arrangement. Your index finger is Lennon and your middle finger is McCartney!

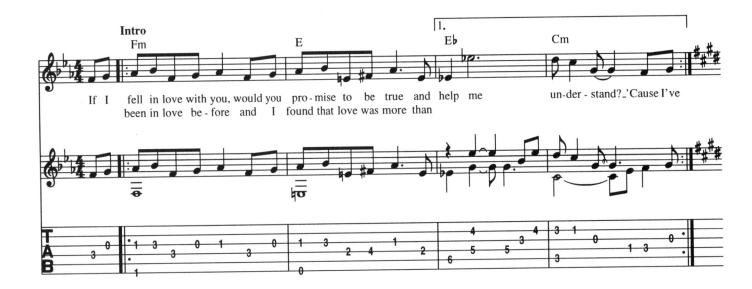

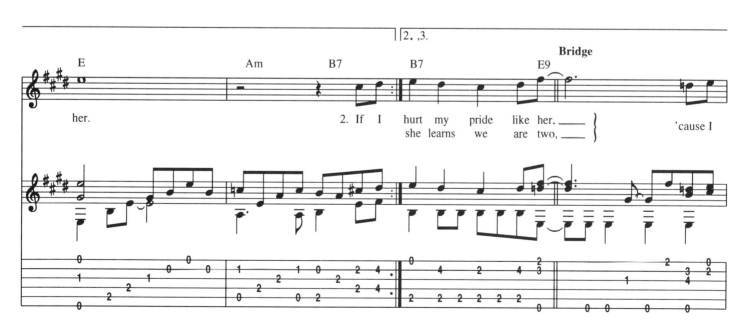

could-n't stand the pain, ___ and I ___ would be sad if our new

love was in vain. 3.,4. So I she learns we are two. ___ If I

fell in love with you. ___

Strawberry Fields Forever

Words and Music by John Lennon and Paul McCartney

Here are some unusual chord shapes:

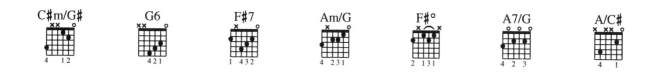

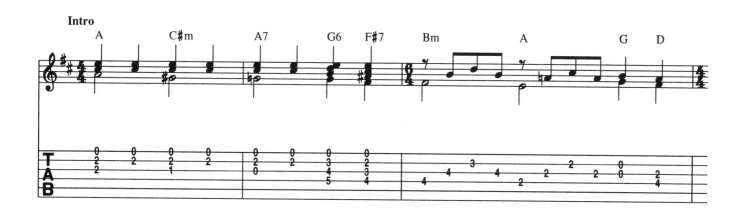

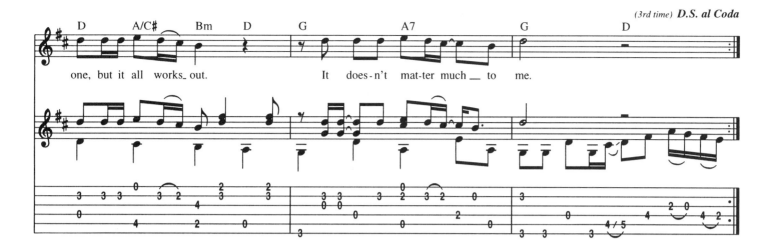

⊕ *Coda*

Additional Lyrics

2. No one I think is in my tree, I mean it must be high or low.
   That is, you can't, you know, tune in but it's all right.
   That is, I think it's not too bad. *(Chorus)*

3. Always know, sometimes think it's me, but you know I know when it's a dream.
   I think I know, I mean, ah yes, but it's all wrong.
   That is, I think I disagree. *(Chorus)*

Lucy In the Sky With Diamonds

Words and Music by John Lennon and Paul McCartney

The opening chord progression (A, A/G, F#m7, F+) is really a major chord (A) held over a descending bass line, which is a characteristic Beatles sound. It happens in "Michelle" and "While My Guitar Gently Weeps" with a minor chord, in "Hey Jude" and "Strawberry Fields Forever" with a major chord, and in "Something" with minor and major chords. Make sure you are familiar with these chord shapes:

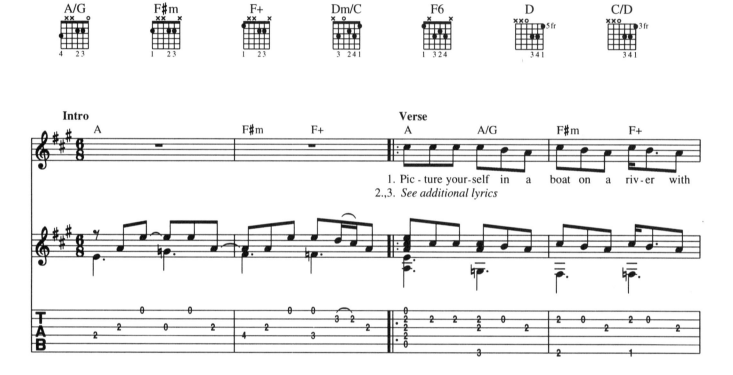

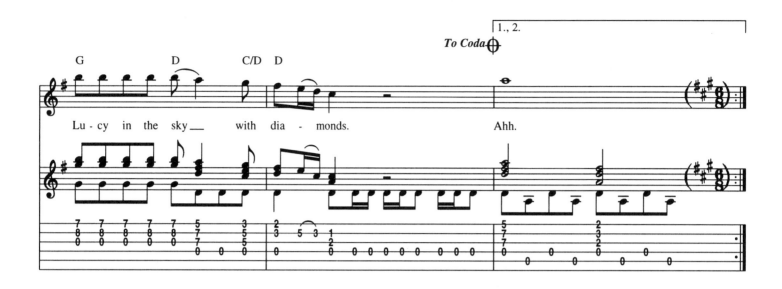

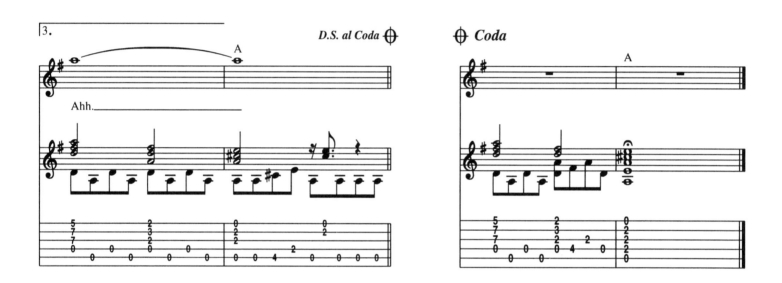

Additional Lyrics

2. Follow her down to a bridge by a fountain,
   Where rocking horse people eat marshmallow pies.
   Everyone smiles as you drift past the flowers that grow so incredibly high.
   Newspaper taxis appear on the shore, waiting to take you away.
   Climb in the back with your head in the clouds and you're gone. *(Chorus)*

3. Picture yourself on a train in a station with plasticine porters with looking-glass ties.
   Suddenly someone is there at the turnstile, the girl with kaleidoscope eyes. *(Chorus)*

Hey Jude

Words and Music by John Lennon and Paul McCartney

There are many three-note chords in this arrangement that are really two notes plus an open bass string (see measures 3, 4 and 5 for examples). The key of A is perfect for this type of playing, because of the open E, A and D bass strings.

MCA music publishing

⊕ Coda

Outro

Additional Lyrics

3. Hey Jude, don't let me down, you have found her, now go and get her.
   Remember to let her into your heart, then you can start to make it better.

   Bridge
   So let it out and let it in. Hey Jude, begin.
   You're waiting for someone to perfrom with.
   And don't you know that it's just you, hey Jude, you'll do.
   The movement you need is on your shoulder.
   Da da da da da, da da da da.

4. Hey Jude, don't make it bad. Take a sad song and make it better.
   Remember to let her under your skin, then you begin to make it better,
   Better, better, better, better, better, oh.

Come Together

Words and Music by John Lennon and Paul McCartney

The drop-D tuning is used often by blues, folk, country, and rock guitarists because the low D bass note sounds so good when you play in the key of D. The Beatles used it on "Dear Prudence" and "Mother Nature's Son."

This arrangement includes some unusual chord shapes, such as this barred G7:

The intro lick may be easier to play if you barre the top four strings, like this:

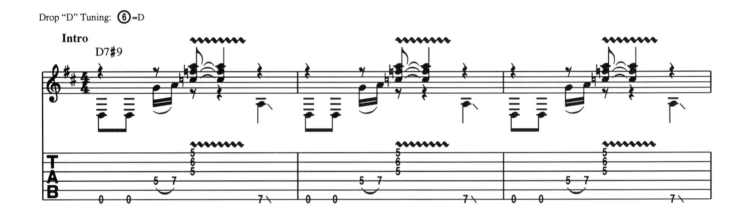

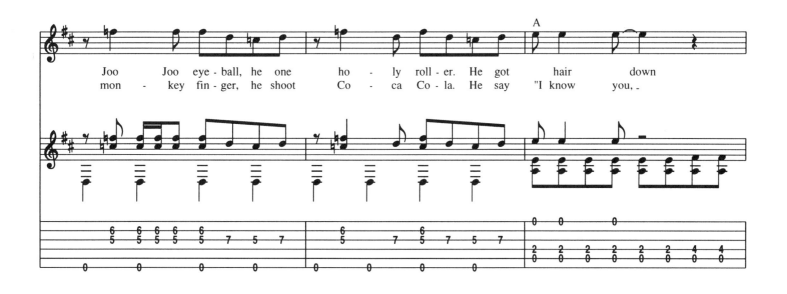

Joo Joo eye-ball, he one ho - ly roll-er. He got hair down
mon - key fin - ger, he shoot Co - ca Co - la. He say "I know you,

to his knee. Got to be a jok - er, he just do what he please.
you know me." One thing I can tell you is you

3rd time, D.C. al Coda

Chorus

got to be free. Come to-geth - er, right now, o - ver me.

⊕ **Coda**

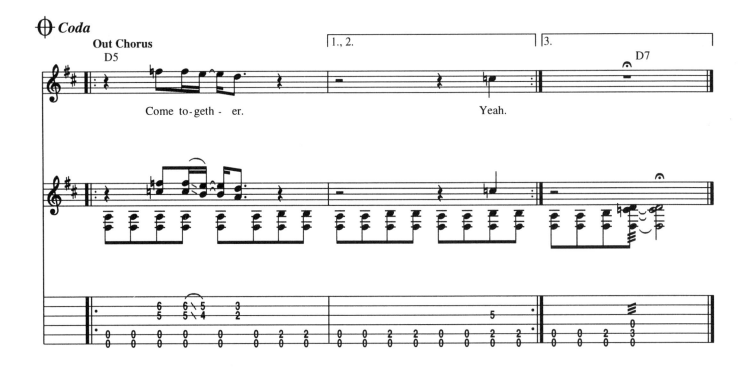

Additional Lyrics

3. He Bag Production, he got walrus gumboot,
   He got Ono sideboard, he one spinal cracker,
   He got feet down below his knee.
   Hold you in his armchair, you can feel his disease. *(Chorus)*

4. He roller coaster, he got early warning, he got Muddy Water, he one mojo filter.
   He say, "One and one and one is three."
   Got to be good looking 'cause he's so hard to see. *(Chorus)*